The Group Process

Field Guide

A Juvenile Detention Based Program

By: Chad Sharpe

JMJ-BOSCO 1911 Publishing Inc.
2215 Chesaning Rd
Montrose, MI 48457
jmjboscopublisher1911@gmail.com

ISBN 978-1-365-65063-5

JMJ-BOSCO 1911 Publishing Inc.
2215 Chesaning Rd
Montrose, MI 48457
jmjboscopublisher1911@gmail.com

Ordering Information:
Quantity sales. Special discounts are available on quantity purchases by corporations, associations, and others. For details, contact the Author at the address above.
Orders by U.S. trade bookstores and wholesalers. Please visit Lulu.com and search for the title and/or the Author

The cover and the art work within this book was done by the youth at G.V.R.C. (Genesee Valley Regional Center) and the Buckham/GVRC Share Art Project.

Contents

INTRODUCTION:

The Group Process is a detention based program that is similar to Group Guided Intervention (GGI) module and Positive Peer Culture (PPC) module. The Group Process module has evolved from over 25 years of application in a working environment and flourished into a highly successful program. The Group Process foundation was taken from PPC and GGI and developed into a program that works very well in a high secure juvenile detention center. Nonetheless, it continues to change and strengthen to accommodate ever changing policies and practices, and it exposes problems, harmful behaviors, and issues. It is a process and a function that the group uses to "help" one another solve those exposed problems and address the behaviors harmful to others in a respectful caring manner. Staff observation of the individual youth and the group as a whole is an important requirement and skill. It requires staff to communicate with each other and develop strategies that promote a positive philosophy within the group. Ultimately, it requires staff to make caring "fashionable" by conveying a positive set of values and a belief that the group has the capability to actually help each other solve problems.

"If you can't convince them, confuse them."

-Harry S. Truman

ACKNOWLEDGMENTS

Long before the Group Process field guide was written, colleagues provided influence, lengthy discussions (with multitudes of old training handouts) and sparks that formulated an idea. I am indebted to Michael Cardwell, Tim Waterson, Steven Kleiner, and Michael Gagnon for the influence and the ideas that they provoked through their answers to endless questions. For ideas to develop and grow into something tangible, the environment must be favorable. For a favorable environment, the leadership must be impeccable and dedicated to the program and the youth we serve as much as our Executive Director at Genesee Valley Regional Center (G.V.R.C.), Fredrick Woelmer. I am as indebted as I am fascinated with his ability to create an agency wide environment in which ideas become realities.

"If the highest aim of a captain were to preserve his ship, he would keep it in port forever."

-Thomas Aquinas

The art within The Group Process Field Guide was done by the youth at Genesee Valley Regional Detention Center (GVRC) through the Buckham/GVRC Share Art Project, which was started in the fall of 2011 through a grant from the Ruth Mott Foundation, brings visual arts, theatre, dance, and spoken word poetry workshops to the youth at GVRC. A collaboration between the Buckham Fine arts Project and GVRC, the Project currently conducts workshops 3 nights per week.

The Project's goal is to introduce artistic concepts and techniques to youth as means of creative self-expression as well as a vehicle for self-exploration, social skill building, and positive peer interaction through the Group Process.

The students at GVRC are proud to share their hopes, dreams, inspirations, and creative works with the public in an exhibit at Buckham Gallery and in the book and video *Let Your Voices Be Heard.*

-Chad Sharpe

Part 1
The Staff

"We cannot solve our problems with the same thinking we used when we created them."

-Albert Einstein

Chapter 1
Staff Involvement & Awareness with the Groups

Involvement & Awareness

All staff must be (or become) "of good judgment" observers of human behavior as it manifests itself in both the individual and the group. Staff will eventually become masters at watching body language and interactions between the youth. Of course, these are skills that require practice and patience, and will develop over time.

Of equal importance, is that the staff must be aware of the attitude and tone or each individual group member and group, as a whole. Staff must also realize what different variables change the tone of the group. They will use these observations later in their documentation, updating on coming staff, and information sharing during staff team meetings. Identification of the maturity level of not just each youth but the group as a whole, becomes a useful tool for the team staff to create meaningful individual or group strategies.

Special documentation should be taken of any unusual, inappropriate, or intense feelings or behavior of a student toward others or himself (self-concept). Staff should take clear notes for information sharing when these situations surface. Staff will ultimately develop awareness for sub-groupings of the youth that they are managing. Being aware of these groupings will help the staff team develop stage appropriate strategies and discern a clear idea of the groups and/or individual developed stage within the program.

Listed below are the sub-groups that staff should observe and document.

Individual Sub-groupings that staff should be aware of

A. **The General** - The negative indigenous leader or the youth attempting to gain control of the group with negative behaviors. The staff role is to get him/her to cooperate with the program and use their leadership skills positively.

B. **The lieutenants** – Supporters of the "General." Remove or suppress the lieutenants support and the "General" tends to lose power.

C. **The follower** – The follower tends to follow the direction of whomever they perceive as having the power in the group.

D. **The fence sitter** - This individual has not made up their mind who to follow or support. They are usually struggling between positive and negative leadership.

E. **The scapegoat** - This is the youth that is made to bear the blame of their group members, and at times, the entire group.

The staff should be continually aware of the sub-groups. The general positive and/or negative tone of the group (caring and helping vs. delinquent and hurting) must be monitored at all times and documented in the wing log as a group summary. Meaningful, and precise observations as outlined above should be documented along with alternative solutions. These are the skills which will need continuing development, and are essential to the effectiveness of proper programming.

While functioning as an observer of human behavior, the staff is called upon both to make judgments about the behavior and to take action based upon those judgments. The interaction, process or tone among the group must be a helping, caring, enabling, positive force. **Nothing else is acceptable.** This force is referred to as the group "culture or Core".

"You must be the change you wish to see in the world."

-Mahatma Gandhi

Chapter 2

THE TOP 10 WAYS STAFF GET INVOLVED

1. **Staff Responsibility**-The staff carries the responsibility for maintaining the positive process by nurturing the positive core, and encouraging program growth within the group. The staff gives guidance to solving and/or identifying problems. However, this responsibility is carried throughout the group. It is not uncommon for staff to take a "Cheerleader Role" as the group is moving through the developing stages. When the group becomes more mature within the program, this role like many others, are assumed by the group.

2. **Put it back on the group**-Continually, the problem is placed back on the group for their consideration and action. Staff can stop the group at any given moment to have them address problems and behaviors. Staff, completely aware of the group's maturity level, will help the group identify the problems by asking

open ended questions. Based on the maturity level of the group, the staff can determine if the group can handle the issue or hurtful behavior of an individual peer. Most importantly, every issue or problem is reintroduced back to the group for discussion. In some cases a youth will approach staff with a problem with a peer or the entire group. Staff will generally stop the group and inform the group that their peer has a problem. The staff, again depending on the group's maturity, will help guide the youth and the group on appropriate and safe ways of dealing with the issue. In some cases the group will be proficient enough to have meaningful dialogue about the issue.

3. **Demanding change 1.0**-If group structure is not in a positive form, then the group needs to be confronted with this issue, demanding change to facilitate the desired positive tone. This might require staff intervention. Eventually, most groups will work very hard to detour staff from having to intervene on group matters.

4. **Staff intervening**-At times, staff must intervene directly to achieve the desired change. Even then the problem is put back upon the group, forcing attention to the group's lack of action in

dealing with the problems, and motivating them to take responsibility and positive action. The same format is true in dealing with individual behavior. The group should continually be aware of the behavior of its individual members, but if at any particular time they are not, then the staff should immediately stop the group and help them identify the hurtful behavior by asking the group a series of open ended questions that will extract the issue. Staff should always make it know that it isn't the behavior that has the staff attention, but how well or how poor the group handled the situation.

5. **Give the responsibility to the group**-The staff should not take the responsibility away from the group to help one of its members. In fact, the group should dread the thought of staff "running" their group when they are given the power to govern their own group as long as they follow the program rules, policies, and guidelines.

6. **Demanding change 2.0**- The group must be forced into this role if they hesitate to take action themselves. The staff team should develop strategies that will encourage and force a caring culture. Strategies could range from the entire group, and

individual, or a combination of both. The strategy should be for the betterment of the group. Staff need to be attentive that creating a positive core within the group does not work with pushing the group with negative strategies. Negative directives will never develop positive outcomes when working with delinquent youth.

7. **Staff stepping in**-As a last resort, if the group absolutely refuses to confront a group member, the staff should step in and initiate appropriate controls. Even then the problem is redirected back to the group for appropriate handling. The group then needs to be confronted on why they did not help one of their group members.

8. **Setting limits**-If the group does not maintain control of its members, staff must set limits to maintain control. Staff should set limits that are enforceable, reasonable, and within the agencies policies. Staff should also be aware of any strategies developed by the team for the group. A "time out" for example can render quite useful. Having the group or individual take a "time out" for a short period of time (no more than 30 minutes) will allow for the

group to gather its composure and focus on having an appropriate talk.

9. **Temporary Measures**-The staff's limit setting is only a temporary measure, and should always involve the group members.

10. **Never stops**-Again, it is a continual process of maintaining the positive "culture" or core. Always look for learning situations for the group and encourage positive interactions regardless of the situation.

"To improve is to change; to be perfect is to change often."

- **Winston Churchill**

Chapter 3

PROGRAMMING GROUP INVOLVEMENT:

Staff member should implement projects, activities, team building sports, etc., which will constantly keep the group involved in types of interactions that demand creativity and responsibility of group members and which gives, as well, opportunities for problems to surface, and the group to intervene as they occur.

The focus must be on activities that do not divide the group into individuals with nine youth doing nine different individual activities, unless at the same time they must function as a group to accomplish these nine different activities.

Below are a few activities that keep the group on focus;

A. Team building activities

B. Team sports in recreation

C. Play writing

D. Orientation of new peers/group or develop games to teach the program

E. Program games to teach the process

F. Give the group the responsibility of making decisions i.e., holiday schedule, recreation schedule, etc. (more mature group)

G. Cleaning the wing/gym/pod/bathrooms etc…

H. Be creative!!!

The staff must convey an involved caring attitude. However, the staff should not become so engrossed as to be unaware of what else is going on with the group. This is an opportunity for staff to observe any of the sub-grouping discussed earlier and/or any cliques that have positive or negative influences within the group. However, the staff member is not a guard or policeman whose function is to remain standoffish while maintaining control by giving orders, but, as a professionally helping and observing individual who also guides the group process.

Team building activities and games have helped groups open up more and start discussing problems and/or developing solutions that have been suppressed. It is not uncommon for detention based groups to function as "casing out groups," "limit testing groups," (these developing stages will be discussed later) or simply an immature group. In these cases, the staff needs to be more creative. Staff should consider the youth who have been in the program for a while. Generally these individuals know the rules and are capable enough to teach them to their peers.

"If everyone is moving forward together then success takes care of itself"

-Henry Ford

Chapter 4

Staff Roles and How to Work Them

Staff should develop and practice playing specific roles while guiding the group process. Staff should be able to change their role based on the situation at hand. It is preferred and not uncommon for a veteran staff to switch from a manager role to a nurturer or vice versa when the need arises. When staff lacks the insight or ability to switch roles from situation to situation, problems could arise that greatly impact the program progression. Below is a list of roles that staff may play depending on a particular situation. Each role has a communication style and possible outcomes if the staff lacks the ability to change roles.

I. Manager role- the staff is responsible for administrative duties related to his/her position and interpreting facility and wing rules, explaining them to the juveniles, and ensuring that these rules are followed, including giving consequences for broken rules. <u>Communication Style: Direct, firm, clear, and task-orientated. The</u>

negative: Staff becomes overly direct and does not allow the youth to learn, use, or follow the program without constant direction. The group generally become more defiant and resists the program and staff directions. Staff will become targets of the negative acting out. The group will have a negative demeanor and will, at first, be quiet. Tension will rise and youth will resist. Staff will take the "watch dog" or "guard" stance with the group and become punitive when group resistance develops. In fact, staff might be lecturing and over talking issues with the group.

J. Counselor Role- The staff helps the group to resolve their problems in an effective manner by utilizing open ended questions and/or reflective speech. In most cases a veteran staff is able to effectively listen to and direct a group or an individual to a beneficial outcome by asking well composed guiding questions. Communication Style: Supportive, understanding, guiding The negative: Staff tends to solve problems for youth and the group without utilizing the group. Staff could be seen pulling youth to the side and doing "one-on-ones" with youth that are having issues or problems that should be brought to the group.

K. Teacher role- The staff provides instructions, direction and support for learning of the program. The object of utilizing this role is for staff to instruct the youth to teach the program, rules, and process to the new youth. Communication Style: Clear, specific, patience, educating. The negative: If the staff over teaches, they generally lose focus on when the group knows the program. Staff will provide instructions and directions when the group clearly knows what to do during most situations. The best teacher to a new peer is another youth in the group that knows the program and has the ability to teach the program. Staff will usually assign this youth as a mentor to the new member of the group.

L. Nurturer role- The staff acts similar to a parent by encouraging and supporting the youth. As mentioned earlier, staff will take the role of a "cheerleader" and encourage the group by praise when they do well or show disappointment when they do inadequately. Once the group takes over this role, the staff will back off and let the group members proceed independently. Communication Style: Caring, supportive, guiding, patient. The negative: Staff can become overly supportive and will generally want all the youth to like them. In extreme cases, some staff will want the group to accept them as one of them, as a member of the group or another adolescent. Personal boundaries and all regard for safety are jeopardized. Staff can put themselves in a dangerous position if they attempt to seek approval and/or acceptance from the group. Staff in this circumstance might allow group members to break rules and "walk" over their authority.

In such activities as sports, the staff should be involved to the extent of picking the captains and seeing that the teams are picked; being the umpire, referee, etc., or seeing that certain group members are given that responsibility, and monitoring the whole activity. Even when the need comes up that staff can and should become involved in the group's activity they should be reserved and aware of the individual and group dynamics.

Activities must not sanction hurting behavior. Any activity that glorifies hurting, such as boxing that have no value as a sport or skill, should be banned. It is counter-productive to the whole tone of helping and caring for one another.

TAKING INTEREST IN THE INDIVIDUALS AND THEIR ENVIRONMENT:

Develop relationships, but know when staff should be "less relationship and more task orientated" or "More relationship and less task" with the groups.

Knowing and learning stages of development to help in assessing groups and developing stage appropriate strategies will provide staff with an unbelievable advantage. In brief, when the group is in the early stages of development they are referred to being "Casing Out." Staff's role is to direct and tell them what to do, teach them how to teach the program, give the group instructions and see how they carry them out. Staff should be able to point out to the group what they did right and what should be corrected by the group. As the group matures and grows, the group will develop to a stage known as "Limit Testing," where they tend to challenge authority, support negative behaviors, and start questioning the rules and staff directions. As the group matures they become more polarized and the helping process becomes more positive and accepting. The group will deal with problems or group conflicts with positive values. And finally, the group will mature into a high functioning group that will require very little staff help or intervention. (Vorath & Brentro 1985)(See Assessing Group and Developing Stage appropriate Strategies Appendix A)

Staff should show concern about all health, hygiene, and medical problems. Showing concern about personal needs such as clothing and other necessary personal items (Staff can say comments such as," I like our wing to look good."), this will show the youth a positive role model. Besides, if the youth trust that you care for them, then they will normally render trust towards you. See that the unit has adequate supplies and has a high level of cleanliness.

It is important to know if the youth is a gang member, has friends in the program, or has codefendants. Use information like this to place a new youth into a group. Make a special note of the problems individuals present and what progress a student is making in the solving of those problems. Utilize this information when developing plans or strategies to help a group improve or to see if an individual youth will make a good mentor. Be careful about confronting or counseling a student on an individual basis.

This could prove as a mistake, especially when the youth will come to you with every problem or issues looking for a solution.

How the groups should handle problems and how staff should guide this process.

Youth are expected to point out negative, harmful behaviors throughout the day. If they do not, staff should stop the group, circle them up and ask the group: "Group what just happened?" It is important that youth understand they are expected to point out these behaviors in order for the group to deal with them and proceed. A youth should say what the behavior(s) were and staff should ask if anyone has anything to add, or if the group agrees with the comment. Staff should ask open ended questions of the group: "How did that make you feel?", "Group, how was that harmful?", or "Group, can you explain to Jimmy how it was harmful." Do not ask too many "WHY" questions. The impact of the behavior should be discussed. Do not allow the group to keep repeating input. If you feel they did a good job ask them, "Can anyone explain how the group did at discussing this problem," "Are you satisfied with how well the group gave input?" If yes, tell them they did a good job, and handle the youth, if needed, from there. What is desired is for the negative/harmful behavior to stop. Do not ask the group if they accept the input for the person that showed the behaviors. The most important thing is to stop the behavior. If it is negative or harmful; the youth does not have to agree that they showed the behavior, only that they hear what the group is saying. The issues can/should be brought up later in Group Meeting, where problems on the subject can be worked out if needed. If this is a repeated behavior, and the group is having a hard time dealing with it, staff may want to remove the youth from the group till the youth is more willing to address his/her behavior. Also, staff needs to be sure that the youth has the maturity to realize and change his/her behavior. In most cases the group should be told to continue to point out behaviors. It is alright to tell the group that not everyone is the same, and we will do what is best for the group and individual. It is important that the group feels protected and supported by staff. In some cases it may be appropriate to write out a restriction for a youth that continues to show hurtful behaviors toward the group or their peers. Group input has to be part of this plan. The idea is to point out behaviors, supported or not, and help the group make it through the day until issues can be talked out in group meeting. If the group cannot handle something then staff will have to deal with it at that time, utilizing the group and teaching problems solving. Every problem, issue, and crisis should be seen as a learning opportunity.

Allowing staff to have power through the groups

Staff should feel empowered and comfortable enough to place a youth on restriction and remove a youth from restriction. If necessary, remove a youth from having up-level status. In fact, staff should have a voice in team meeting on deciding appropriate group and individual strategies.

Staff needs to understand the concept and program outline. If staff doesn't know the basics of the helping process, then you can never expect the youth to know the program. Frequently, good staff teams review and discuss the program guidelines and how the helping process is working.

Successful strategies require that all staff follow the strategies developed and agreed upon by the staff team. Even staff filling in for the regular staff needs to know the plan.

Understanding and adjusting to any situation requires the staff to be able to assess their assigned group. During staff team meetings, staff will need to develop working strategies that are stage appropriate and realistic for the groups. More importantly, staff needs to follow the strategies.

"Progress is impossible without change, and those who cannot change their minds cannot change anything."

-George Bernard Shaw

Part 2
Techniques the Positive way

"Step with care and great tact, and remember that life's a Great Balancing Act."

-Dr. Seuss

Chapter 5
Effective & Ineffective Group and Individual Strategies

TECHNIQUES FOR ACHIEVING A POSITIVE CULTURE:

The most important element for achieving a positive culture is the degree of care and concern or respect among not only the youth within the program, but the staff that oversees the group.

The staff can only produce a caring group by themselves respecting the youth and role modeling appropriate behaviors and attitudes. Staff should encourage care and concern often and help the group to identify when care and concern were demonstrated by the group.

Common sense and common courtesy are basic in working with the group. Staff members who lack one or both of these attributes tend to struggle managing this type of program. While expectations must be high, which means expecting the young person to ultimately be totally responsible and totally self-sufficient, the expectations must not be absurd or ridiculous. At all cost, the program needs clear and concise policies that cover programming and operations within the unit. Staff should have a comprehensible understanding of program policies and procedures that directly deal with limits and guidelines for any and all activates on the unit. Staff should take it upon themselves to refresh their knowledge of these operation policies and should be encouraged to participate in updating and writing polices that could improve the unit's performance.

Specific Techniques

Specific techniques to use in building a positive "culture or core" in the group process should be encouraged and utilized during team meetings and day-to-day activities. Staff should be encouraged to follow the teams strategies for the group and/or individual youth, but should also be encouraged to "think outside the box" when building a positive group. Again, any and all strategies should be brought back to the staff team for discussion and approval, and to insure that staff is on the same page. Below are a few techniques that have been proven as useful tools in building positive groups and a positive core.

1. **Utilizing Positive Strength** – This technique is used to motivate group members to achieve a more positive "culture or core." Example; The youth point out and draw out the care and concern in whatever manner or fashion it is shown, no matter how slight it may be. Staff can circle up the group when a peer or several group members show care and concern or respect. Staff might use open ended question such as, "Can anyone explain to me what just happened?" After the group members identify the care and concern staff should praise the group and the individual(s). This technique can and should be used frequently, especially when the youth has used the process correctly.
2. **Neutralizing Negative Influences** - An example of this technique would be when the group is working with Joe to help him see his problem, and John is negatively supporting Joe, then John may have to be momentarily removed by being placed in another room with another staff member. After that, they can work with John and his need to hurt Joe. This is one approach. In other instances another approach may be necessary and more

effective. <u>Remember:</u> A group can usually work with only one group member and one problem at a time. It may mean setting aside all but the most basic and urgent problem simply by closing off all comments, expressions, and side-chatter about anything but the primary problem or issue. Once the caring "culture or core" gains strength, then some of the side problems and influences can be handled by the group members with support from the staff. However, only staff can remove a peer from the group for a limited time-out. Therefore, staff needs to be observant enough and have good enough judgment of the group to remove the youth. Generally, staff bases their actions on the maturity level of the group in dealing with the specific problem or issue.

3. **Disorientation** –This technique is to be used only long enough to achieve a desired result. When a group member(s) are trying to gain negative control over the group, by second-guessing the program, manipulating the routine, predicting staff responses, or encouraging peers to not follow the program, schedule, or rules of a particular activity, staff should make the routine unpredictable. Example: A youth has been giving help and showing negative leadership but the group says nothing nor gives him any help. A

movie night is planned. When it is time to go to the movies, only the above youth goes and the rest of the group remains back. When the youth ask why, you may reply – "Don't you know?" When the group asks what is happening, you may say, "You people should know…" Staff should help the group realize that they are supporting the negative behavior. The object is to have the group identify and figure-out the issue without staff giving up to much information. Once the group starts holding that peer accountable, staff should consequence the negative indigenous leader. This technique takes away the "General's" and "Lieutenants."

4. **Reversal** -This technique is one that must constantly be ready for use whenever the group or any of its members try to make their problems or responsibilities someone else's fault. Since the delinquent is good at avoiding responsibility for negative behavior (because to admit it means to face the feelings and issues behind it) he initially tries to avoid it by making others feel responsible for his behavior. The reversal technique simply places the accountability back in proper perspective.

Ineffective strategies

In some cases strategies are not to be taken as the best or only technique for a desired change. Each situation is unique and must be approached uniquely and creatively, and with an ultimate concern for the young people and their benefit. Staff should take a deep look at how the strategy is affecting the individual, the group, the staff, and the unit as a whole. In some cases staff teams will attempt to incorporate a strategy into the program because it was found to be useful for one particular challenging youth. From my observation supervising a staff team, a strategy of this nature will generally receive a name or identification. Here are a few warning signs that staff should be aware of.

M. "**The Same old thing"** – It is easy to get into a rut and draw from the same short list of strategies. The strategies may be fine, and at one time were effective, but repetition and predictability rendered them useless.

N. **Punitive** - Punitive strategies usually do little to advance the group process. They can create antagonistic feelings between peers and between peers and staff. Punitive measures generally do nothing to teach and develop competency in the group members.

O. **Individualized** – Sometimes we are tempted to develop strategies for one particular youth in a way that does not involve the whole group. It takes creativity to think of the group as the client and create a culture in which youth are involved in helping each other. Sometimes youth provoke us to want to take over for the group rather than involve them as expert helpers.

Twelve Strategy Development Questions

This list of questions might help the staff team determine if the strategy they are using has been helpful or is in need of tweaking. Avoiding ineffective strategies will help the unit and the youth groups to flow smoothly. Answering these questions could help the unit manager redirect the staff team from making the blunder of a useless approach to an infectious problem.

TWELVE STRATEGY DEVELOPMENT QUESTIONS

1. What is the present group culture?
    a. Who helps/who hurts?
    b. What does the rest of the group think of them?
    c. Who gets support? Confrontation?
    d. How does the group handle day to day responsibilities?
2. How is this different from last week?
3. What did we want to accomplish with this group last week?
4. What was our strategy?
5. Did we use that strategy?
    A. Explain how it was done?
    B. If we didn't do it, why?
6. Did the strategy work?
    A. Wholly or in part?
7. What do we want to accomplish next week?
    A. Who needs to help more?
    B. Is the group supporting positive or negative behaviors?
    C. Who is the positive leader/Negative leader?

D. What goals can the group accomplish?

8. What can we do to get the group to achieve these goals?

   A. Who needs support and how?

   B. Who needs confrontation and how?

   C. What opportunities for intervention are likely to arise this week?

   D. Can we create opportunities for success?

   E. Who can be held accountable for others behaviors?

   F. What specific values can be emphasized?

9. How are we going to do the above?

   A. Who will do it?

   B. When will it be done?

   C. How can all staff be involved in their own ways?

   D. Need for coordination?

10. What might happen to change this strategy?

    A. What alternatives are there?

11. How can success be measured?

12. Will everyone support this strategy?

Individual Youth Strategies or Plans

In some cases a youth might require special attention from the staff and the group. Whether they struggle with mental health problems, aggressive behaviors, or both, a staff team might create an individual youth strategy that will help the group, the youth themselves, and staff manage their actions. These plans should be developed by the team staff and reviewed at every team meeting and updated as need or adjusted. This will require staff to observe and measure and document the effectiveness of the plan.

Below is an example of a team developed individual strategy/plan. Jimmy was a youth that was very limited cognitively and acted out sexually inappropriate towards females.

Example: Jimmy's Individual Program (Team reviewed 8/9/2011)

1. Jimmy should be in <u>staff line of sight at every moment</u>. If staff must leave the area he should tag along.
2. He is not required to use the group process. Based on staff discretion, <u>staff may want to keep Jimmy attached to them</u>

throughout their shift. Jimmy tends to do better with one-on-one attention.

3. Jimmy's leisure time activity should be monitored. This means staff should control and manage what he reads and watches. Jimmy enjoys reading the Michigan Chiller books.
4. If he becomes sexually inappropriate he should be removed from the group on a **time out** that lasts until he is under control. Staff should reframe from talking to him until he has calmed down. Jack (up-level) is allowed to give him input unless staff has determined that he is appropriate enough to listen to others, or the group is mature enough to talk to him.
5. Jimmy responds better if he is removed from his audience. Just because he is making verbal sexual threats does not mean that he has the intention to act on them. Therefore he should not be placed on BMT (Behavioral Management Time-out) unless he has shown the intention to do physical harm to others.
6. If Jimmy is placed on wing restriction staff should keep him busy with activities such as sweeping, mopping, or cleaning the wing, an assignment will not work.
7. Jimmy should sit next to staff's table during meals. He should also be required to sit in front of the class room so staff can monitor him. If required, he can sit out in the hall of the class room at a desk.

8. If Jimmy's medications are making him tired and his behaviors are starting to escalate, jimmy can go to bed at 8:00pm (Incident Report is required). **(added 5/24/2011)**
9. ~~If Jimmy has appropriate behaviors which include no inappropriate sexual behaviors staff will bring him in an extra snack on Tuesday. If his behavior continues to be appropriate staff will give him a candy bar on Saturday. This will continue Saturday to Tuesday, then Tuesday to Saturday~~. **(example on how we remove items and change strategies each week)**

Example: Jay's Special Program

If Jay displays any of the below behaviors he will be placed on this special program

1. Threats
2. Attempts of intimidation
3. Playing around/horse play/not following program rules
4. Going off or blowing up when the group attempts to help him with his behaviors
5. Sneaky behaviors (including gang comments and gang signs)
6. Not following staff directions

Jay will be on the floor away from the group for 90 minutes. He will write an assignment about his behavior(s) he displayed. Within the assignment he will address how it was harmful to him and his group. (Nothing else)

He will not come off the wing in that 90 minute time frame and will follow the wing restriction guidelines. The 90 minutes will start as soon as he starts following the guidelines of wing restriction.

If he does poor within the 90 minutes he will remain on the wing for another 90 minutes with the group's encouragement (the group will give him input). He should be encouraged to behave reasonably during the 90 minutes.

When he returns to the group he will be in full program until he does the above behaviors again.

Staff will document his progress in the group summary by noting why he was placed out of program, and if needed, when and why he continued with another 90 minutes

Any school worked missed while he is out of program will be done during his free time at a chair on the wing.

Start date: 7/3/2014

What to Look For In the Groups

In all human interaction there are two major ingredients –content and process. The first deals with the subject matter or the task upon which the group is working. In most interactions, the focus of attention of all person is on the content. The second ingredient, process, is concerned with what is happening between and to the group member(s) while the group is working out the content. Group process deals with such items as morale, feeling tone, atmosphere, influence, participation, style of influence, leadership struggles, conflict, competition, cooperation, etc. In most interactions in our daily lives very little attention is paid to the process, even when it is the major cause of ineffective group action. Being aware and having a keen sensitivity to the group process will better enable one to diagnose group problems early and deal with them more effectively. Being mindful of these processes as they present themselves in the groups, staff will enhance their worth to the staff team and ultimately to the groups they work with. In summary, it's not so much the content that the staff should focus on, but the process in which the group dealt with it.

Below are some observation guidelines to help one process analyze group behavior.

Participation

One indication of involvement is verbal participation. Look for differences in the amount of participation among group members.

- Who are high participators?
- Who are the low participators?

- Do you see any shift in participations? E.g., highs become quiet; lows suddenly become talkative. Do you see any reasons for this in the group interactions?
- How are the silent youth treated? How is their silence interpreted? (Consent, disagreement, disinterested, fear etc.)
- Who talks to whom? Why?
- Who keeps the ball rolling? Why?

Influence

Influence and participation are not the same. Some people may speak very little, yet they capture the attention of the whole group. Others may talk a lot but are generally not listened to by other members.

- Which members are high in influences? That is when they talk others seem to listen.
- Which members are low in influences? Others don't listen or follow them.
- Is there any shifting in the influences?

- Do you see a rivalry in the group? Is there a struggle for leadership? What effect does it have on other group members?

Styles of Influence

Influence can take many forms. It can be positive or negative as we discussed earlier; it can enlist the support or cooperation of others or alienate them. How a person attempts to influence another may be the crucial factor in determining how open or closed the other will be toward being influenced. Below are suggestive of four styles that frequently emerge in groups. Again, observing these styles will help the staff to develop appropriate strategies.

- Authoritarian: Does anyone attempt to impose his will or values on other group members or try to push them to support his decisions? Who evaluates or passes judgment on others members? Do any members block action when it is not moving the direction they desire? Who pushes to "get the group organized?"
- Pacemaker Who eagerly supports other group member's decisions? Does anyone consistently try to avoid conflict or

unpleasant feelings? Does a member of the group "gives others the power?" Do they avoid giving negative feedback or will only give positive input or "candy coat" the behaviors?

- Slacker: Are any group members getting attention by their apparent lack on involvement in the group? Does any group member go along with the group decisions without seeming to commit himself on way or the other? Who seems to be withdrawn and uninvolved?
- Leader: Does anyone try to include everyone in a group decision or discussion? Who expresses his feelings and opinions openly and directly without evaluating or judging others? Who appears to be open to feedback and criticisms from others input? When feelings run high and tension mounts, which members attempt to deal with the conflict in a problem-solving way?

Task Functions

These functions illustrate behaviors that are concerned with getting the job done, or accomplishing the task that the group has before them. These task could be hygiene (shower) time, wing clean up, or even a Group Assistance.

- Does anyone ask for or make suggestions as to the best way to proceed or tackle a problem?
- Does anyone attempt to summarize what has been covered or what has been going on in the group?
- Is there any giving or asking for facts, ideas, opinions, feelings, feedback, or searching for alternatives?
- Who keeps the group on target? Who prevents topic-jumping or going off on tangents?

Maintenance Functions

These functions are important to the morale of the group. They maintain good and harmonious working relationships among the members and create a group atmosphere which enables each member to contribute maximally. They insure smooth and effective teamwork within the group.

- Who helps others get into the discussion?
- Who cuts off others or interrupts them?

- How well are members getting their ideas across? Are some members preoccupied and not listening?
- How are ideas or concerns rejected? How do members react when their ideas are not accepted? Do members attempt to support others when they reject their ideas?

Membership

A major concern for group members is the degree of acceptance or attachment in the group. Different patterns of interaction may develop in the group which gives clues to the degree and kind of membership.

- Is there any sub-groupings? Sometimes two or three members may consistently agree and support each other or consistently disagree and oppose one another.
- Do some youth seem to be 'outside" the group? How those "outside" are treated?
- Do some members move in and out of the group, e.g., lean forward or backward in their chairs or move their chairs in and out? Do they find ways to be separated from the group? Under what conditions do they come in or move out?

Feelings

During any group discussion, feeling are frequently generated by the interactions between members. These feelings, however, are seldom talked about. Observers may have to make guesses based on tone of voice, facial expression, gestures, body language, and many other forms or nonverbal cues.

- What signs of feelings do you observe in group members?
- Do you see any attempts by group members to block the expression of feelings, particularly negative feelings? How is this done? Does anyone do this consistently?

Norms

Standards or ground rules may develop in a group that control the behavior of its members. Norms usually express the beliefs or desires of the majority or who the group perceives as having control. These norms may be clear to all members, known or sensed by only a few, or operating completely below the level of awareness of any group member. Some norms facilitate group process and some hinder it.

- Are certain areas avoided in the group (e.g., talk about present feelings in the group or discussing the up-levels behaviors etc.)?
- Are group members overly nice or polite to each other? Are only positive feelings expressed? Do members agree with each other to readily? What happens when members disagree?
- Do you see norms operating within the questions that are allowed? Do members feel free to probe each other about their feelings? Do questions tend to be restricted to intellectual topics or events outside of the group?

"Success is not final, failure is not fatal: it is the courage to continue that counts."

-Winston Churchill

Chapter 6

How the "Help" is given

Giving help in this program is a process and should be in the complete and natural form of care and concern. If it is used or supported as a negative process to gain control or isolate a peer member then the program is misused and should be pointed out not only by the group, but by the staff when the group fails to witness or address the problem. Equally, if a staff member supports a youth in using the program harshly or as a weapon, the staff should be counseled quickly. Even if the process is used incorrectly, like on a behavior that does not violate a rule, as long as it is done with respect and in a total helping manor, then the process was not misused. Staff should go to all lengths in promoting care and concern when the helping process is used on any behavior or violation of a unit rule.

In most cases learning the rules of the program and how to use the helping process is not the difficult task for the new youth, but how to display care and concern when giving someone help and how to accept it when someone is helping them. However, during the learning of the helping process, some youth will sound robotic in their dialog. This is generally a problem that is rooted from the staff teaching the group how to teach others how to give help in a caring fashion. The helping process is and should be done in the following manor. 1. If a peer sees another peer breaking a rule or doing any behavior that is harmful to another peer, he/she should simply tell that person that they need to stop the behavior or check into stopping the behavior. This might ignite questions from a newer peer about why the behavior is wrong, and should be explained whenever time permits. If time does not permit, then the peer who gave help can tell them that he/she will explain the rule at the next free time. 2. If the behavior continues, then the youth who gave the first help will pass the help to another peer in the group to address the problem or issue. He/she will simply remind them that the behavior needs to stop so that the peer doing the behavior doesn't get in trouble and receive a consequence. 3. If the behavior continues, then the peer who gave the pass help will ask to circle up and run a group assistance (G.A.). However, in certain situations any member of the group can ask the staff to "circle up," or "run a concern." This is usually done when an issue of great importance is at hand and the group needs to address it. The issues will range from two group members arguing or progressively becoming aggressive, to plotting an escape attempt. In some cases, usually with an immature group, staff may stop the group and "circle" them up when he/she sees a behavior that the group is not addressing. The staff will simply ask the group an open ended question such as, "Group, what is the problem, "or "Group, can anyone tell me why I might have circled you guys up?" Open ended questions such as these will help the group process what they have observed and how it was harmful to the group and/or the individual. Again, staff should take this opportunity to encourage and teach the use of the group process. At every opportunity staff should put the issue back on the group for consideration and utilize this time to help the group learn the program through the use of care and concern. In some cases the staff might take into account the number of repeated behaviors and consequence the youth(s) for the destructive behaviors. Staff should see this as a chance to promote growth and change in the youth. Consequences should be meaningful and helpful. Assignments during the loss of free time should require the youth to think about his or her harmful behavior. The peer group is expected to follow the existing rules and guidelines of the facility, but staff should always use the group as the first means of intervention to address negative peer behaviors, that is, to get the group to respond to their group members by pointing out negative behaviors. The object is to get this young person to be responsible for their behaviors through the group intervention. If the group doesn't confront the behavior, staff should take action to stop the negative behavior and motivate the group to take action to address negative behaviors. When a peer is showing the need for help, the group should stop whatever they are doing and offer them help. If the peer repeatedly refuses to accept the group's help and suggestions on how he may control his behaviors, the staff must take the responsibility for that youth and consider if the youth will require a consequence for the repeated behavior(s).

Group Assistance Outline (basic)

Even a Group Assistance (typically called a GA) is done in a formal circle up. When a group is running a GA the youth will generally stand in a circle with their hands to their sides and listen to the input and comments made within this short meeting that resembles a short burst of a group meeting. It is important that the group members know how to run a GA and the importance of running one correctly. A GA should be allowed to run at any time of the day. In some cases, based on the overall maturity of the group, staff should be aware if the GA is being given in a helping manor or a hurtful manor such as when the group is using it to "scape goat" a peer. A helpful remedy for this problem requires staff to ask specific questions to get to the root of the GA and draw out the problem so that the group can identify how it may be harmful. Staff might ask questions such as "who gave the first help," "What behaviors did they show," and "Who did the help get passed to?" This is a teachable moment for the group. The staff may want to address the group on how calling a false GA disrupts the group and is hurtful to the group as a whole. On the other hand, the staff should take every opportunity to praise the group when they call a helpful GA and do a good job running it. Staff should focus on how the group was helpful or harmful rather than the behavior itself. Negative behaviors can always be dealt with, but it's when the group show maturity and positive growth that staff want to praise the group and in some cases an enthusiastic praising is desired and will encourage the group to build further.

Example:

1. The group will circle up
2. The youth running the GA (generally the youth who called for the GA or whomever staff assigns to the task) will state, "My peer Jimmy is receiving a G.A. for using profanity."
3. Next the youth running the GA will ask for any "positive peer input?" Several peers may raise their hands and give input. The input should be focused on the topic and how it was or could have been harmful to the youth himself and/or the group. The group and staff should make sure that the input is not repeated.

4. The youth running the GA will "cap" the GA by saying, "If you have a problem with this GA bring it up in group meeting."
5. Staff Input: staff should critique the GA and focus on how it was ran. Some dialog can be about the behavior, but should be focused around how the group is trying to help. This is also an opportune time for staff to praise the group. In many cases a simple, "you guys did a good job!" will suffice or sometimes a more dramatic praise is in order. However staff might need to consequence the behavior of the youth by saying something like, *"You guys did a good job running this GA and calling out Jimmy's behaviors, but it is a repeated hurtful behavior and I am going to have to consequence Jimmy."* At this time staff will have to set an enforceable consequence for Jimmy.

Below are examples of behaviors that are handled through the group intervention and behaviors handled through direct staff intervention. However, it should be noted that even the behaviors that staff directly handle, the group should be involved. If the youth is out of the program for any issue, the group should be encouraged and allowed to give that youth encouraging input. In most circumstances, encouragement received from other youth tends to be accepted by the youth better.

PROBLEM BEHAVIOR USUALLY HANDLED THROUGH GROUP INTERVENTION

A. Failure to maintain health care
Not taking daily showers, care of hair, brushing teeth, changing clothes daily, improper use of hygiene supplies

B. Failure to maintain living area (Wing)
Failing to clean and maintain personal rooms, participate in Wing clean up, properly using equipment supplies

C. Use of offensive language or gestures
Use of verbal remarks or physical gestures directed toward others that are threatening or insulting in nature

D. Provoking individuals into misbehavior
Misleading others into misbehavior by challenging, daring, gossiping, etc.

E. Disruptive behavior
Causing disturbance through horseplay, excessive noise, pushing, etc.

F. Unauthorized gambling or trading
No trading or gambling for food (snacks, desserts, etc.), personal possessions or County property

G. Defacing property
    No writing, carving or otherwise destructive behavior toward the property of others

H. Verbal aggression toward staff and peers
    No threatening or derogatory remarks to staff or peers

I. Failure to follow GVRC/WING policy
    Ignoring or disregarding GVRC and Wing policies

J. Self-harm
    Cutting or scratching parts of the body, tattooing, or any otherwise harmful behavior

K. Stealing
    Possession of articles belonging to others without permission

L. Contraband
    The possession of any unauthorized articles

M. Non-participation in program
    Failing to participate in program without staff permission

N. Inciting group misconduct
    Any overt (or covert) act intended to disrupt the order and safety of program

O. Leaving supervised area without staff permission
    Not obtaining staff permission before leaving any area

P. Failure to follow staff orders

Not responding to staff directions

Q. Interfering with staff duties

Entering office without permission, disrupting staff's efforts to counsel youth, distracting staff's attention from problem situation

PROBLEM BEHAVIOR HANDLED THROUGH DIRECT STAFF INTERVENTION

(But still utilizing the group)

A. Refusal to accept group intervention (help)

a. Not responding positively to group intervention

B. Group support of negative behavior

a. Refusal by group to correct behavior that is harmful to peers or the group process

C. Assault upon staff or peers

Any physical act that could be harmful to a staff person or peer

D. Weapons

Possession of any item that could be used in a harmful manner

E. Sexual misconduct

Any unlawful sex act

F. Non-Participation in program

Failing to participate in program without staff permission

G. Inciting group misconduct

Any overt (or convert) act intended to disrupt the order and safety of program

H. A.W.O.L. (escape)

Leaving the building without permission, demonstrating a clear intent to truant by plotting or preparing material to truant

Staff should allow the group to address most problems behaviors initially for the purpose of resolving and correction. When and if the group completes this task and if it is accomplished successfully by the group, staff should complement and support the group for its endeavors. Staff should always be there to assist, guide, direct and monitor situations where the group is giving help to its peers to ensure that the group is functioning and participating in a helping, positive manner. If a youth is not being supportive, he should not be allowed to participate or be removed until the matter is resolved. At this time, the group should focus on the individuals who were not supportive in a positive manner one at a time.

It is paramount that staff utilize the peer group as a first means of intervention in addressing and/or resolving negative behaviors. Staff are to evaluate the group to determine the most appropriate intervention for correction of the behavior. In some cases the youth may need to take a "time out" away from the group in order keep from escalating the situation. This can be staff directed or requested by the youth. A "time out" should be encouraged as a non-punitive tool and should be promoted as not a consequence. In most cases, if the youth took a time out, as soon as they return to the group, the group should circle up and discuss the problem. It is important for staff to keep in mind that unless each youth has significantly contributed to the problem through their negative behaviors or attitude, staff team should not evoke a group consequence. Every attempt should be made to identify early individual group members with problems so they may be dealt with individually.

Staff should be cognizant of the level of development of each individual and peer group to develop staff team strategies to respond to the group/individual behaviors. Stages of development will be discussed later in the manual.

In many cases, based on the group's maturity within the program, the staff should allow the group to manage themselves and provide assistance, support and guidance, whenever necessary.

"Mistakes are always forgivable, if one has the courage to admit them."

- **Bruce Lee**

"I urge you to help each other save your souls by good example and advice."

- **John Bosco**

Part 3
Starting and Continuation of the Program

Chapter 7
Sturdy Staff Teams

Develop sturdy staff team(s)

Developing a staff team requires knowing each members strengths and weaknesses. Every person working with the groups on a regular basis are members of the team and should be treated as an active member. This includes youth specialists, teachers, supervisor, group leaders, counselors, nurse, and/or any person actively working with the group on a regular basis. If a staff member is out of work for a long period of time, the staff filling in should be welcomed to the team and respected as a decision making associate. Any decisions should be made as a consensus with all members agreeing on one outcome, whether it is an individual youth plan, group strategy, or schedule for a holiday weekend. As much as we expect the youth groups to develop, great staff teams will generally develop over time and will resemble a high functioning team.

STARTING THE PROGRAM

Getting staff to "Buy" into the program

For most of the staff working in a helping program such as a Group Process Program, seeing results tend to be the main determination and force to developing positively functioning groups. Once a staff sees the difference between a "High Functioning Group" and a "Limit Testing Group," the staff will start taking a more active role in developing groups that work. When staff is asked why they like "high functioning groups" opposed to a "limit testing group," they generally say they do less redirecting and the stress is reduced. Once the staff learn the program, and start allowing the program to work, they start seeing results and start encouraging the youth. Staff then instinctively start encouraging, developing, and nurturing the positive "core or culture". They feed the positive and teach the groups how to neutralize the negative. In fact, this becomes a norm in a seasoned staff team and strategies generally start focusing on individuals rather than the group as a whole.

Developing a daily schedule that is detailed and well thought out is an essential start for a new program. Involve the staff team in making a schedule that gives times and locations of almost every task. Once the schedule is formalized and agreed upon, insure that the youth and staff are following it regularly. Only in the case of an emergency, and/or directed by the wing supervisor, deviations from the schedule should be agreed upon by the staff team. Staff should encourage the youth to learn the schedule and adhere to the timetable. The schedule should be posted for the youth and staff to refer to it when needed. New youth can carry a copy of the schedule and for reference when moving to a new task. Seasoned youth will help new youth follow the schedule during their first time being a line leader. (Note the Schedule Example Appendix G)

The staff team should develop criteria that help the staff and the youth recognize a youth that is showing positive leadership and should be rewarded for their excellent behaviors and leadership for his or her group. Staff will review each youth that requests the privilege of up-level. Staff will make a consensus based on the criteria and the youth's behaviors. Prior to the scheduled staff team meeting, the group should talk about and review all individuals who write up or apply for the honor of being an up-level. Staff can utilize the group's input to make their decision on the nominations for up-level. Nevertheless, it is important for the manager or supervisor of the unit to help the staff team focus on the up-level criteria rather than choosing a youth based on favoritism or because the youth is trying. The criteria should be used in a strict manor. Many times staff will agree that they want the youth to show "one more week" of meeting the up-level criteria, but should keep in mind that this can only be used once. Ensuring that staff give specific behaviors or criteria to strive for are important in developing the up-level candidate. "Wishy-washy" agreements will only cause later disagreement within the staff teams and youth groups. It can be helpful and educating when the staff team invites an up-level candidate into their meeting for an interview and/or an opportunity to explain in detail what the young person is needing to adjust to earn the status of an up-level. Opportunities like this will eliminate later problems and questions between the staff. With that being said, any and all up-level privileges should be strictly for up-levels. Any deviation from this will only cause problems among the youth and lessens the value and impact of the privileges for the up-levels who have earned the elite honor. (Example of Up-level Criteria Appendix C)

Team meetings are where the staff team discusses the progress of the groups and combine their information for the bi-weekly progress reports for individual youth, decide on group recommendations for up-levels, and plan effective strategies for their groups. This is done on a weekly basis. Each youth reviewed that week are usually notified during group meeting on how they are doing based on the approved rating system of the facility. Youth might receive a list of behaviors that staff suggests they improve. However, it is more effective for the group to point out the behaviors with staff agreeing and supporting them. Youth on suicide watch are reviewed by the staff to determine if he or she should be escalated or de-escalated. Each and every issue within the group, the wing or pod, the program, and even the staff need to be brought up and talked about. An experienced team will automatically bring up topics to address staff problems or issues, even if the problem is a failed attempt to follow a developed strategy. This means that you, as the staff member, bring in their observations as you see the groups function in their settings, listen to the observations of other team members, help plan out how to achieve certain objectives with the group or individuals in your settings and contacts. Also, this is the place for all the staff of that team to work through their differences which interfere with the effectiveness of the team's strategies. (Example of Team Minutes Appendix F)

Managing New Youth

When a new youth enters the program they receive the same privileges that all others receive. For example, all youth that are in the program and not on a restriction will have T.V. time between 7:00pm-8:00pm. This should be a standard privilege and should only be lost if the individual or in some cases the group lost this privilege. Many times throughout the day the groups will circle up and discuss a problem or run a group assistant that will run over into a set privilege. It is important for the youth and staff to realize that the program supersedes any and all activities and problems that need to be discussed come first. Again, Up-levels should receive items that are clear incentives for being a positive leader in the program. For example an up-level might receive a DVD player in their room at night, game station access, MP3 player during free time, stay up later, longer visits and phone calls, or even a special visit where their family is allowed to bring them in food. Whatever the privileges are for the up-level, they should clearly supersede the normal standard privileges that all youth within the program receive. The Team staff in many cases can approve extra up-level privileges that are outside of the normal up-level incentives. For example, an up-level from another wing/pod can have recreation time with his sibling on a different wing/pod.

Once the program is developed, the staff team should work out a method for the youth to teach the program. Some programs use a pamphlet or a flash card system given to each youth. It is important for the group to know and understand that the new peers are their responsibility and they are responsible to orientate them and teach them the program rules. Any system is useful only if the youth are able to understand it and teach it to their new peers. Staff teams can design a standard way in which a new youth is orientated by their group members. Orientation is very critical to the success of a group and the new youth. Staff should take a very small role in this process. Staff, if anything, should demonstrate how to orientate rather than orientate the new youth. Staff role could be testing the new youth, but even in this case a mature group could take this responsibility. Staff's main role is observation and guiding if needed, especially if the group has a tendency to make up new rules or are simply limited in the program or process.

(Example of a Youth Orientation Pamphlet Appendix H)

TEN BASIC BELIEFS FOR PEER GROUPS

1. Youth are greatly influenced by associations with peers.
2. The peer group can be used to solve problems.
3. A problem is an opportunity to learn.
4. As a person gives and becomes of value to others he or she increases their own feelings of worthiness and builds a positive self-concept.
5. Rebellious and strong willed individuals, when redirected, have much to contribute. Those who have encountered

many difficulties in their own lives are often in the best position to understand the problems of others.

6. It is more important to teach basic values than to impose specific rules.

7. Caring means wanting what is best for a person.

8. Youth often think that negative, harmful behavior is more "cool" than positive caring behavior

9. These same youth can be taught to see that caring behavior is "cool".

10. People seldom will be more responsible than they are expected to be or more helpful than they are allowed to be.

"It takes courage to grow up and become who you really are."

- e. e. cummings

Chapter 8
Communication

COMMUNICATION – THIS IS VERY CRUCIAL:

Communication is crucial in this type of program. It is important for all staff to read the wing log and initial what they have read. They must log in the wing log book all pertinent information concerning the group and group members, even though it may seem like a small thing at the time. If they notice anything of significance about other groups, be sure the other group's staff receives the information so that it is entered into that wing log. Verbal communication between teachers, wing staff, supervisor/group leaders, and other staff is essential. It is vital that when one staff relieves another for a shift or group, they spend a few moments alone with each other to share information about things that are to be followed through and the immediate condition of the groups and their members. Here is an example of a good group summary.

Date: 7/2/14

3:30pm Group 1 Summary

The group seemed to struggle this shift, nothing major; however there were a lot of out bursting during class when they should be raising their hands for questions and a lack of care and concern within the group. During Art class they "all" seemed off focus with the out bursting and too many peers were up and not doing their work. After lunch in the canteen room Jimmy and Carter were at odds. Carter handled himself well. Jimmy was threatening to punch someone (indirect threat towards Carter). The group circled up and discussed the issue with Jimmy. He later calmed down. In the afternoon during Basic education class I left the group with Mr. "C" for two minutes to take medications to intake. When I returned Jimmy and Henry were going back and forth. I calmed down Henry quickly, but had to send Jimmy down the hallway for a time out. He later talked out his frustrations with several of his peers and was later able to return to the group. He continued to struggle with his class work. Throughout the day there were developing issues and a poor attitude by Jimmy. Watch for Ken coming out of his shell. He was very hyper today and overly playful. Allen stayed awake in class all day and did his school work. Carter circled up the group and the group gave him praise for doing so well.

"Intelligence, knowledge, or experience are important and might get you a job, but strong communication skills are what will get you promoted."

-Mireille Guiliano

Part 4
Running Group Meetings

Chapter 9
Group Meeting Basics

RUNNING GROUP MEETINGS

Group meeting reviews the day and should be seen as the most important part of the day. The meeting should be the outlet for all issues and problems that occurred throughout the day. The youth should be able to bring their concerns to the meeting and talk about them openly and respectfully. The meeting should follow a format that is reasonable and that can be learned and followed daily. Group meeting should be ran at the same times every day and the group members should be set up and ready for the staff. Likewise, the staff should be on time and ready to observe the group. The meeting should last 90 minutes and no longer. Group meetings are youth facilitated and should remain that way. Staff should take a guiding role only, but can ask open ended questions that will bring out issues that the group might be over-looking. Many times during the meeting staff should remain quiet and observe how the group is handling a particular issue or problem.

Staff needs to remember that this is the group's time to discuss issues. If the group does not utilize the entire 90 minutes, the staff could have the group come up with an activity that involves each group member. At times, groups might require staff to assign them a team building activity that will take up the remainder of the time. Staff should be aware that groups will attempt to "fly" through the meeting only to receive free time or avoiding issues. When this happens, staff should review with them the meeting and have them talk about problems that occurred. The youth should know that problems and issues that occurred from that day should be brought up. The group should not be allowed to bring up old issues, unless they are still occurring.

THE GROUP MEETING

The Importance of Group Meeting

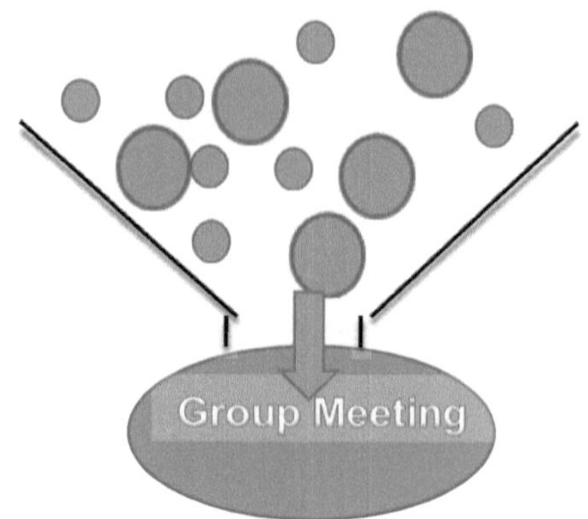

All problems and issues should be brought up to the group during the meeting. In some cases an issues maybe "capped" until group meeting. Any concerns, problems, and GA should be brought up for later discussion. NO matter if the problem was minor or large, the group should review the outcome and the youth should have an opportunity to discuss the issue appropriately with his/her group. This approach should be done in a caring manor. If the group is unable to address the issues respectfully, the staff should stop the group and coach them in a correct direction. This may take several times and will require patience. It is not uncommon for the group to stop the meeting to review how to respectfully confront an issues/problem.

"If your brother sins (against you), go and tell him his fault between you and him alone. If he listens to you, you have won over your brother. If he does not listen, take one or two others along with you, so that every fact may be established on the testimony of two or three witnesses. If he refuse to listen to them, tell the church (congregation)."

-Matt. 18:15-17

Chapter 10

Detailed Group Meeting

Group Meeting Outline

The youth group leader (youth) will start the meeting out by reminding the group of the "group meeting expectations." Expectations seem more acceptable to the youth than group meeting rules and are generally followed. Examples of the expectations are basic rules such as, "be respectful to your peers," or "Don't repeat input."

Group Goal: The group will work out problems using group help and care and concern with yourself and others. The group leader will read this goal before the meeting. Each person in the group will make eye contact and commit to the goal. If eye contact is not made, the group leader will repeat the goal.

The group leader will then ask the following questions to each person in the group;

1. Any communication? Communications from anyone outside of the facility, Probation officer, Case worker, counselor, parents etc… This is an opportunity for the youth to talk about anything that is upsetting them.
2. Any problems or Behaviors of the day, or how was your day? The youth being asked this question should talk about any problems that they might have had within the program or with a

peer. The youth might simply refuse to say anything, which is fine. This portion of the meeting allows the youth to get issues out in the open.

3. Group Help, who wants to give some suggestions of encouragement? Youth in the group will raise their hands and give input to this peer. More mature groups normally don't raise their hands to give input without interrupting others. The input should be with care and concern. If a youth is harsh, and the group does not address it, staff should say, "group, what is the problem here?" All input should be caring and helpful to the youth, but should also address issues and problems or behaviors. The group leader will allow everyone to participate, but will not force them to give input. If the input is repeated, the group should inform the peers with care and concern and move on. If behaviors are not pointed out, then staff should ask, "What about this…or that…"

After each person in the group goes through the above three questions the youth group leader will move on to the next four questions.

4. Does anyone have any issues with the input they were offered? At this point, youth who had a problem with the input they received or an intervention (help) from the day are able to express their concern. Youth might go back and forth on the issue, but it should be respectful. It is helpful to have the group members raise their hands and take turns. In mature groups, the youths in the group will take the role of the mediator.

5. Who wants more help or encouragement with their issues of the day? The group as a whole should agree on who receives more "helping" input. Staff should be aware if it is the same youth being singled out each group meeting and redirect as needed. Staff should ask the group opened ended questions to get the group to pick a youth that might benefit from the input that day.

6. What can the group do to improve? (open discussion) This is the most important portion of the meeting. The youth have an opportunity to discuss, develop, plan or even strategize. Staff can help the group in developing a new group goal, or define where the group is going and how they plan on getting there. This portion of the meeting usually takes about 45 minutes, especially in a functioning group.

7. Anyone wants to change their goal or has a concern? The group members agree and change their goals. In some cases a youth might need to work on his goal further, whereas others might have completed their goal. At this point, the youth in the group should help that person come up with a goal that will help him improve in the program. Again, this is a group task and staff should only guide as needed. A skilled staff can ask leading questions that will help the youth and the group pick a useful goal. In some circumstances asking a simple question like, "What do you need to work on in order to earn your up-level" or" Is there a goal you think you might be able to accomplish?" Opened ended questions are found to be helpful when guiding a youth to a new individual goal.

8. Staff Input? The staff should summarize the meeting, or ask the group questions to help them process how they are doing and positive experiences they have had throughout the day. In some cases staff might say something along the lines as, "I don't have anything to say, you guys took my thunder. You said what I wanted to say. Good Job group." This is also an opportunity to praise the youth who don't normally participate.

Group meeting should be comfortable for the youth, but structured enough that the routine will continue for years. Sometimes, staff might start the meeting asking one exploring question that leads into a 90 minute discussion. Creativity will help the groups achieve successful group meetings. (Note the Group Meeting Outline for the youth Appendix F)

CONCLUSION:

While the standards and expectations of youth by all staff must be high, they must also be realistic. We are not attempting to make "choir boys and girls" out of the youth, but rather our goal is to make adequately functioning, positive individuals who can "make it in the program on a day to day basis" without resorting to further delinquent anti-social behavior. Detention is too short term for a complete treatment quality program, but when a program such as the Group Process is utilized it promotes a treatment twist to detention that just might provide the ultimate bonus of changing a life.

Appendix A

Assessing Groups and Developing Stage Appropriate Strategies

Casing Out: A new group or a group in transition after a change in membership characterized by guarded, tentative, and untrusting behaviors

Group's Behavior

- Silent
- Sitting back and watching; analyzing
- Stalling
- Letting things happen
- Questioning for information (what if…?)
- Provide little information about self
- Don't make waves
- No risk taking
- Plays dumb and innocent
- Blame others
- "Honeymoon" period
- Compliant and generally cooperative
- Some youth will try to avoid the group and deal with staff one-on-one
- Some youth will withdraw and try to do as little as possible

Staff's Strategies

- Teach what, when, who, and where by showing and demonstrating
- Be specific in directions and instruction, focusing on teaching and encouragement, even for small accomplishments
- Give the group continual feedback on their progress

- High staff interaction, especially during problem discussion.
- Staff makes the majority of decisions
- Staff Role model behaviors
- Stress listening
- Set time frames and demand that youth meet expectations
- Provide close guidance and supervision to ensure emotional and physical safety
- Increase individual and group responsibility as youth show the ability to handle it
- Relationships within the group are encouraged while relationships with staff are minimized

Nature of staff involvement: High Task/Low Relationship

The most crucial stage for group development. If negative norms are allowed and take root, it is difficult to change them later on

Assessing Groups and Developing Stage Appropriate Strategies

Limit Testing: Group is adapting to new environment with unchanged values and inappropriate behaviors.

Group's Behavior

- No pride in the group
- Do not like each other and are against each other as wall as staff
- Test limits to see how much they can get away with
- Show and provoke problems with each other
- Make up rules and then change them to suit what the youth in power want
- Project blame for their actions on others
- Keeps problems/issues underground
- Do not trust anyone, each youth is "out for themselves"

- Brag about negative behaviors
- Use the excuse of "playing" when they are really aggravating or hurting others
- Use the program to hurt others
- Unwilling to show genuine feelings
- Have great difficulty achieving any group goals
- They are vying at times for negative leadership
- Gravitate towards those they perceive as being in power

Staff Strategies

- Catch group doing things right and give praise and recognition in the form of more decisions making power
- When they make poor decisions, let them experience the consequence of their actions. Debrief to help them find out where they made a poor choice
- Before giving them responsibility, make sure they have the knowledge and experience needed for success. Do not set them up for failure.
- Structure and provide success experience
- Stress care and concern for group members
- Provide firm consistent consequences for hiding or denying negative behaviors. Treat negative behavior that is being dealt with as a learning tool. Show disappointment in hurting and dishonest behavior.
- Show confidence in their potential for improvement
- Teach and model respect for one another.

Nature of staff involvement: High Task/Low Relationship

Assessing Groups and Developing Stage Appropriate Strategies

Positive Polarization: Positive and negative forces interacting within the group.

Group' Behavior

- Group is starting to give help in a caring fashion
- Some individuals will attempt to support staff
- Some combinations of group members can be trusted to do what is right.
- Individuals in the group are trying to take over the "Cheerleader" role that staff had assumed to this point
- Starting to have some group identification
- Individuals start to trust others in the group
- The negative leader starts to have some anxiety about losing his grip on the group
- The negative lieutenants start to feel pressure and question their alliance to the negative leader(s).
- Individuals in the group start to take personal risks and work on real change
- The group may start a project or task in a reasonable manor, but fall apart due to opposing forces
- The negative leaders are often successful at pulling down the positive leaders due to lack of positive support
- Many group members are "fence sitters" going the way of whoever is in power
- At the beginning of polarization, the positive youth may backslide due to pressure
- In the later stage of positive polarization, the pressure falls on the negative leaders.

Staff Strategies

- Allow the group more opportunity to make their own decisions, teach group members, and give help. Monitor their input and reward appropriate efforts.
- Continue to expand their areas of decision making as they show maturity
- Continue to praise but in more restrained ways

- Carefully monitor the group, and examine and support the youth that are trying to do the right. If the youth are "fronting" or "faking" continue to encourage them.
- Do not clamp down too hard when the group makes poor decisions. Debrief and process poor decisions, and let the group know they are capable
- Provide natural and logical consequences for those who support hurtful behaviors
- Help group to identify positive behaviors and support their positive feelings or outcomes
- Limit the use of group consequences while supporting and empowering positive fractions within the group
- Dig for details when explanations are vague
- Find ways to reward positive youth even if there are only a few the group
- Support positive behaviors even when it appears to be "Fake."
- Label problem behaviors as ineffective solutions and assist the group in looking for alternatives.

Nature of Staff Involvement: Low Task/High Relationship

Assessing Groups and Developing Stage Appropriate Strategies

High Functioning: A group that is more independent and takes responsibility for guiding its group members. Mature group.

Group Behavior

- There are enough positive fractions in the group to assure that situations are being dealt with appropriately, even when staff are not around.
- Problem discussions are conducted in a meaningful and caring fashion.
- They are able to connect the learning with their future behaviors in the community
- Shows strong group identity and feel good about their group
- The group has an air of hope and expectation of positive outcomes
- They meet challenges with energy
- They don't fall apart when problems occur and make good recoveries
- There is little anxiety on behalf of the youth that are acting in a positive manor
- Youth that behave negatively feel more anxiety
- Discussions are realistic and complete
- The group focuses on helping youth stop behaviors rather than merely labeling the problem
- Youth are able to stay more consistent because of the positive support they receive.
- The group is aware of all group members and show care and concern when dealing with individual problems
- The group is less rigid in their thinking. Instead they think through each situation

Staff Strategies

- Staff are unobtrusive yet observant
- Staff restrain form guiding discussions and give the group a chance to do it themselves
- Address backsliding by debriefing and reviewing, not by clamping down on the group as a whole
- Allow group to decide their daily operation as much as possible
- Continue to structure challenges and opportunities for success
- DO NOT take positive behaviors for granted. Continue to build, support, and raise expectations

Nature of Staff Relationship: Low Task/High Relationship

(Vorath & Brentro 1985)

Appendix B

Another example of a Special Program

1. Kelly should sit near staff at all events or activities including school and meals
2. It is staff discretion if Kelly will use the group process. With the immaturity of the current group, it is suggested that she is directed by staff only.
3. No special accommodations. i.e.…watching TV rather than recreation or church, sleeping during program hours, or not having to participate in program scheduled activities.
4. Staff will remove her from the group if or when she becomes aggressive or threatening.
    a. Place her on restriction for repeated behaviors
    b. Place her on Behavioral Time Out if she is struggling with de-escalation when she is threatening peers/staff. Kelly is known to get out of control quickly.
5. Kelly generally de-escalates quickly. Staff should isolate her from an audience; this has worked well in the past. Just

because Kelly is down the hall yelling and/or threatening does not mean she needs to be placed in her room. Staff should make the decision of placing her on BMT based on their discretion and the current events. However; make sure she is clearly <u>out of control **and** in danger of harming herself or others.</u>

6. Kelly has an issue touching others, mainly staff. She needs to feel a consequence for this behavior. There is zero tolerance for this behavior.

Appendix C

Up-Level Criteria

1. In the program one week prior to selection.
2. Is a positive peer role model
3. Is an active participant in the group process
4. Uses the group process with care and concern, not to hurt
5. Uses the group process consistently
6. Confronts negative behavior in a positive manner
7. Accepts correction of inappropriate behavior in a positive manner
8. No behavior requiring direct staff intervention and consequences
9. Is a positive peer in school
10. Attempts to do good classroom work
11. Supports staff during group interactions
12. Gives the group good input
13. Knows the schedule
14. Keeps the group on focus

Appendix D Team Meeting Example

Staff Attended: Present Absent

Minutes Submitted By: Time Started

Chair Next Week: Time Finished

Youth Days Behaviors in Program and Rating Next Report Date

(Youth being reviewed with detailed behaviors and any other information that will help the team)

1. Group 1 Strategies:

   (Detailed information and plans on how to handle the group and in some cases individuals within the group)

2. Group 2 Strategies:

Suicide Watch Risk Level Suicide WatchRisk Level

1. (Youth name)

2.

A. Group 1 Up-levels: B. Group 2 Up-levels

1. (Youth name) Yes or No; 1. Yes or No;

2. Yes or No; 2. Yes or No;

A. Group 1 Clothes Room: B. Group 2 Clothes Room:

1. (Youth name) 1.

2. Alt: 2. Alt:

Team Staff/Supervisor Agenda Items

1.

APPENDIX E Flashcards

Where and what do you do when you line up for bedtime?	1. By the showers 2. no talking unless giving help 3. show staff what's in your hand 4. line up in room number order 5. face forward
Name all of West wing staff including teachers	1. Staff Names here
Name 5 extra privileges an up-level receives	Food from the "outs" Wear up-level shoes Extra phone calls Candy MP3 players/DVD players Longer visits Stay up later (10:15-10:30pm) Special visit
What does staff review you on during team meeting?	1. Attitude 5. School 2. Behavior 6. Visits 3. Medical/medicine 7. Hygiene 4. Working/wing behavior 8. Overall review
How do you give help?	1. First Help 2. If first help is not accepted, pass the help 3. If behavior continues, call a G.A.
How long are visit if you're on free time, wing restriction, or BMT?	1. Free time = full 2. Wing restriction = 30 minutes 3. BMT = zero to 15 minutes
What do you do if you have a problem with a peer?	1. Talk to them 1 on 1 2. Bring it up as a concern 3. Bring it up in group meeting
How man hard cover books are you allowed in your room?	None, unless directed by staff for an assignment
What do you do if you want your	1. wait for staff to come down the hall and ask them

light off at night?	2. **NO** yelling out of your room 3. **NO** banging/Knocking
Is "sagging" allowed in the program and how is it fixed?	**NO**, "sagging" (pants below waist) is not allowed. Dropping the pants size will usually fix the problem
How many youth are allowed in staff office?	None
What are the charges for plotting and attempting AWOL (Escape)?	1. Plotting = 2+ years 2. Attempting = 4+ years
What is a positive way to give help?	With care and concern, **Respectful!!!**
Can a group member communicate with the other group or wing?	No, it could start a fight or riot and someone could get hurt.
Is a timeout a consequence?	1. No, a peer could take a time out if they are upset, crying, or need to get themselves together
When is big wing clean up?	Group 1 = Odd Saturdays Group 2 = Even Saturday
What does GVRC stand for?	Genesee Valley Regional Center
Where do you go for a tornado warning?	Down the hall by your room. Sit down, no talking, follow staff directions.
How many people are allowed in the showers at one time?	1. 5 people 3. No staring/Face forward 2. No talking 4. No laughing/giggling
What do you do if a peer is talking about AWOL/Escape?	**NOTIFY STAFF IMMEDIATELY** to avoid charges or other consequences
What is a concern and why would staff or your peers call one?	A concern is a problem in the group. Staff may call a concern when the group has a problem and has not addressed it or given it help
What are the consequences that staff gives?	Loss of canteen, Loss of free time, Wing restriction, and B.M.T. (behavioral management timeout)
How many letters can you send out a week?	1. Two 2. four if you are an up-level
What is the process for sending	1. Address it correctly 2. Give it to staff to examine

out a letter?	
What do you do then you are done eating?	1. Raise hand and ask to scrape 2. return your fork to staff table
How do you handle it if a "help" is passed to you?	1. ask your peer to stop the behavior 2. If they do not stop the behavior, ask for a G.A.
What does a G.A. stand for?	Group Assistance
Is a GA a bad thing?	**NO, it's to help you**
What days does your group have visits?	Group1 = Saturday 3:30pm-6:30pm Group2 = Sunday 12:00-3:00pm
What days does the schedule switch?	Even Saturdays after lunch
What does the towel on the door mean?	It lets staff know there is someone in the room in case of an emergency
What do you do if there is a fight?	1. Sit Down 2. Get away 3. Notify staff 4. Follow staff directions
Name7 of the 13 wing restriction rules	1. 30 minute visit 2. 30 minute recreation 3. No talking to other peers on restriction 4. Up time every hour 5. Raise hand to speak, NO yelling 6. Eat all meals on wing 7. Sit quietly in the area staff tells you
During what showers can you NOT wash your hair?	Morning showers
Who counts the toothbrushes and Sporks?	The last person
What happens if staff finds contraband, books, or magazines in your room?	1. Books and magazines = restriction 2. Contraband = Free time, Wing restriction, or BMT depending on the severity
Can you "throw up" gang signs and why?	**1. NO** 2. They can start fights or riots and someone could get hurt
What staff carries the keys to the outside doors?	**NONE!!!**

How many phone calls do you get a week and when?	1. One on weekends 2. Two if you're an up-level (Thur. and Weekends)
Why do you have to ask to step through the doors?	So staff knows where you are at all times and to keep you safe from other groups or wings
What are the individual goals a peer has?	1. Learn peers name 2. Learn Flash Cards 3. Learn the process 4. Behavioral Goal (given in group meeting)
Why do you carry your fork with you during meals?	1. So someone will not use it to make a weapon 2. So someone will not touch it or spit on it
What does supporting negative behavior mean?	Laughing, following, not giving it help, or agreeing with the negative behavior
When do you get reviewed by staff?	Thursdays
What do you do if you have a problem with staff?	1. Talk to the staff 1 on 1 2. If that doesn't work write a grievance letter and give it to the supervisor
Can you yell out your room at night?	1. **NO!!!** 2. You could wake up on wing restriction or be moved to isolation
What are the steps of Morning Group Meeting?	1. Individual Goals 2. Group Goal 3. Individual Concern 4. Group Concern 5. Staff input/directions
How long are visits?	1. 2 hours 2. 3 hours if you're an up-level
What is appropriate sexual activity at GVRC?	None, sexual activity of any type is prohibited
What do you do if you witness or suspect any type of sexual activity?	Immediately report it by verbal or written notice through the grievance process
How do you keep yourself and others safe? Name 4 of the 7	1. Follow the rules of the program 2. Don't keep secrets 3. Don't isolate with another peer

ways	4. Don't trade food or goods 5. Never accept gifts or promises from another youth in return for not telling on the youth or bringing up issues to the staff or the group 6. Always report and discuss issues with your staff and group 7. Don't enter into romantic relationships with other youths
What could happen if someone knowingly makes a false allegation?	It is a legal violation and charges could be pressed
Can you use the bathroom during visits?	No, you must use the bathroom before your visit or it will be terminated.

Appendix F

Group members commit to the goal

1. Any communication?

2. Any problems or behaviors of the day, or how was your day?

3. Group Members Input

4. Does anyone have any issues with the input they were offered?

5. Who wants more help or encouragement with their issues of the day?

6. What can the group do to improve? **(The Group Goal can be made and changed here. Group should focus on topics that will improve their groups.)**

7. Anyone wants to change their goal or has a concern?

8. Staff Input

APPENDIX G. Schedule Example

MONDAY-FRIDAY

TIME ODD DAYS **TIME EVEN DAYS**

7:00 to 7:30 am Morning Hygiene 7:00 to 7:30 am Morning Hygiene

7:30 to 8:00 am Morning Meeting 7:30 to 8:00 am Breakfast

8:00 to 8:30 am Breakfast 8:00 to 8:30 am Morning Meeting

8:30 to 10:00 am Basic Education 8:30 to 10:00 am Basic Education

10:00 to 11:30 am P.E. Class 10:00 to 11:30 am P.E. Class

11:30 to 12:00pm Showers 11:30 to 12:00pm Lunch

12:00 to 12:30pm Lunch 12:00 to 12:30pm On Wing

12:30 to 2:00pmBasic Education 12:30 to 2:00pmBasic Education

2:00 to 3:30pm VOC Ed-Tech 2:00 to 3:30pm VOC Ed-Tech

3:30 to 5:00pm On Wing 3:30 to 4:30 pm Rec./showers

5:00 to 5:30pm Dinner 4:30 to 5:00pm Dinner

5:30 to 6:30pm Canteen 5:00 to 5:30pm On Wing

6:30 to 7:30pm Recreation/Showers 5:30 to 7:00pm Group Meeting

7:30 to 9:30pm Group Meeting/Bed 7:00 to 7:30pm On Wing

7:30 to 9:30pm Canteen/Bed

SATURDAY

TIME ODD DAYS **TIME EVEN DAYS**

7:00 to 7:30 am Hygiene 7:00 to 7:30 am Hygiene

7:30 to 8:00 am On wing 7:30 to 8:00 am Breakfast

8:00 to 8:30 am Breakfast 8:00 to 8:30 am M.G.M./On wing

8:30 to 11:30 am Big Clean Up 8:30 to 10:00 am Recreation

11:30 to 12:00 pm Lunch 10:00 to 11:30 am Canteen

12:00 to 12:30pm On wing 11:30 to 12:00pm Lunch

12:30 to 1:30 pm Recreation 12:00 to 1:30 pm On wing/Recreation

1:30 to 2:30 pm Canteen 1:30 to 2:30 pm Canteen

2:30 to 5:00 pm visits start 2:30 to 5:00 pm On wing/ visits start
3:30

5:00 to 5:30 pm Dinner/ visits 5:00 to 5:30 pm Dinner/ visits

5:30 to 7:00 pm Recreation 5:30 to 7:00 pm Recreation/ visits end
6:30

7:00 to 7:30 pm Showers 7:00 to 7:30 pm Showers

7:30 to 9:00 pm Group meeting7:30 to 9:00 pm Group meeting

9:00 to 9:30 pm Bedtime 9:00 to 9:30 pm bedtime

SUNDAY

TIME ODD DAYS **TIME EVEN DAYS**

10:00 to 10:30 am Breakfast 10:00 to 10:30 am Hygiene/Breakfast

10:30 to 12:00 pm 10:30 to 11:30 pm M.G.M./On

M.G.M./On wing/Church wing/Church

12:00 to 12:30 pm Lunch11:30 to 12:00 pm On Wing

12:30 to 2:30 pm On Wing 12:00 to 12:30 pm Lunch

2:30 to 3:30 pm Canteen 12:30 to 1:30 pm Canteen

3:30 to 4:30 pm Recreation/ 1:30 to 2:30 pm Recreation

and showers

4:30 to 5:00 pm On wing2:30 to 4:30 pm On wing

5:00 to 5:30 pm Dinner 4:30 to 5:00 pm Dinner

5:30 to 9:30 pm Movies/Bed 5:00 to 9:30 pm Movies/Bed

Appendix H

YOUTH ORIENTATION PAMPHLET

Example

The Detention Center

GROUP INTERVENTION PROGRAM RULES/POLICY

Welcome to Regional Center. We hope the time you spend in detention will be productive and as pleasant as possible. As you read through this program, remember that it serves as a guideline for your behavior while at RC.

During the intake process personal property is inventoried and held by the Center until your release.

Upon entering the wing, you will be issued grooming items and will be assigned to a group. One telephone call will be made, upon your admission, to your parents or guardian.

Rooms, lockers and personal files are searched periodically.

STANDARD GOALS:

While you are in detention, it is important to remember that your behavior is evaluated every two weeks and upon release. These evaluations are based on the following six standard goals. The evaluations are completed during team meeting and sent to your caseworker and placement.

The six standards are:

1. Follow agency and wing expectations
2. Maintain personal hygiene and a clean living area
3. Attend and participate in school
4. Display positive relationships with peers
5. Display positive relationships with staff
6. Participate positively in the group process and realistically address personal goals.

GROUP INTERVENTION PROGRAM

The program at RC emphasizes positive behavior through peer group intervention. Group members are expected to give support for positive behavior and assist in monitoring the behavior of group members. Program privileges are earned by cooperation with the group process and compliance with agency and wing expectations.

GROUP INTERVENTION PROGRAM

All youth are expected to participate in the Group Intervention Program. You will move about in a group and be responsible for your own behavior as well as that of your group. You are expected to participate in the group meeting. You are expected to demonstrate care and concern for your peers and to be an active group member. The most important responsibilities for you during the program day are:

1. Point out to peers that their behavior is or may become hurtful to themselves or other people

2. Ask the person showing hurtful behavior to stop the behavior

3. Help that person to understand how it was a hurting behavior and to accept the responsibility for that behavior

4. Not support the negative behaviors of another peer in any way

5. Listen to and use positive input from peers

Helping a peer identify and change a hurting behavior should be done in a positive and appropriate manner. You should also accept help from a peer positively and appropriately.

Nominations for "Up Level" peers are made by peers during Group Meeting. A peer can nominate themselves for Up-Level. The peer can write why they feel they deserve an "Up-Level" position. The staff team will make the final decision during Team Meeting. Up-Level nominees are reviewed and decided upon each week. If an "UP LEVEL" displays problem behavior requiring direct staff intervention and consequence, youth will relinquish (give up the position) the Upper Level status.

"UP LEVEL" CRITERIA (another example)

1. In program at least one week prior to selection.

2. Is a positive peer role model

3. Is an active participant in the group process

4. Confronts negative behavior in a positive manner

5. Accepts correction of inappropriate behavior in a positive manner

6. No behavior requiring direct staff intervention and consequences

GROUP INTERVENTION PROGRAM

When peers are participating in the RC Group Intervention Program (GIP) and the group and peers are functioning positively and assuming the responsibilities of the peer group, staff are to accord those youth (and group) all the privileges outlined for the peer group program. Youth on restriction will have fewer privileges, while Upper Level youth will have extra privileges.

AGENCY AND WING EXPECTATIONS

1. You are expected to work within the peer group process.

2. You are expected to treat others with respect.

3. You are expected to line up with your group before leaving the wing area in a quiet and orderly manner. There is no talking to peers when line is moving.

4. You are expected to turn in all pencils, markers, hair bands, etc. before leaving the wing area or going to bed.

5. If a fight breaks out, or other emergency occurs, you are expected to move away from the problem and follow the directions of the staff.

6. Towels are to be hung on the bedroom door after your evening shower and used the next morning for your shower.

7. Nothing can be covering the lights or windows in the bedrooms.

8. Pictures may be placed on one wall of your room covering an area of 2 by 3 squares per room.

9. You may be allowed to have up to 2 soft covered books or magazines at night at staff's discretion, but they are to be removed in the morning.

10. You will participate in all activities.

11. You must have staff permission to leave any supervised area.

12. You are expected to follow all of the directions given by staff.

13. Staff permission is required before entering the staff's office, storage rooms, broom closet, etc.

14. In the dining area, you are expected to use good table manners and not waste food. You must take your eating utensils with you any time you leave the table. You may talk quietly if staff gives you permission. If you have any questions you may ask staff.

15. When staff directs the group to have "quiet time" or when a peer is on restriction the group/peer needs to raise their hand(s) and wait for staff to acknowledge them before talking to staff.

PERSONAL HYGIENE AND LIVING ENVIRONMENT

1. You are expected to maintain good personal hygiene. You may wash your hair at night and when showering before special grooming.

2. Sanitary napkins (pads) will be made available to you. They will be in staff's office. You need to inform staff if you need one. Special arrangements can be made if you need more than one at a time.

3. You are expected to properly dispose of sanitary napkins. You will be provided with small bags to dispose of sanitary napkins. Do not flush sanitary napkins down the toilet. Always dispose of used sanitary napkins in disposable bags that are provided.

4. Clothes are issued on second shift. You are responsible at that time for making sure they fit properly and are in good repair. If you need to exchange your clothes, you must do it at that time. If you need a hair band, it will be made available to you in the morning.

5. You are expected to maintain your room and living area in a clean and orderly manner.

SCHOOL

You are expected to attend classes, perform all assigned tasks, and follow the instructions of the teacher (s).

POSITIVE RELATIONSHIPS WITH PEERS

You are to follow the Group Intervention Process Guidelines.

POSITIVE RELATIONSHIPS WITH STAFF

1. You are expected to treat staff with respect and communicate with staff in an appropriate manner.

2. You must sign the appropriate sheet to talk to the nurse.

PROBLEM BEHAVIOR USUALLY HANDLED THROUGH GROUP INTERVENTION

R. Failure to maintain health care
   Not taking daily showers, care of hair, brushing teeth, changing clothes daily, improper use of hygiene supplies

S. Failure to maintain living area (Wing)
   Failing to clean and maintain personal rooms, participate in Wing clean up, properly using equipment supplies

T. Use of offensive language or gestures
   Use of verbal remarks or physical gestures directed toward others that are threatening or insulting in nature

U. Provoking individuals into misbehavior
   Misleading others into misbehavior by challenging, daring, gossiping, etc.

V. Disruptive behavior
   Causing disturbance through horseplay, excessive noise, pushing, etc.

W. Unauthorized gambling or trading
  No trading or gambling for food (snacks, desserts, etc.), personal possessions or County property

X. Defacing property
  No writing, carving or otherwise destructive behavior toward the property of others

Y. Verbal aggression toward staff and peers
  No threatening or derogatory remarks to staff or peers

Z. Failure to follow RC/WING policy
  Ignoring or disregarding RC and Wing policies

AA. Self-harm
  Cutting or scratching parts of the body, tattooing, or any otherwise harmful behavior

BB. Stealing
  Possession of articles belonging to others without permission

CC. Contraband
  The possession of any unauthorized articles

DD. Non-participation in program
  Failing to participate in program without staff's permission

EE. Inciting group misconduct
  Any overt (or covert) act intended to disrupt the order and safety of program

FF. Leaving supervised area without staff's permission
  Not obtaining staff's permission before leaving any area

GG. Failure to follow staff orders

Not responding to staff directions

HH. Interfering with staff duties

Entering office without permission, disrupting staff's efforts to counsel youth, distracting staff's attention from problem situation

PROBLEM BEHAVIOR HANDLED THROUGH DIRECT STAFF INTERVENTION

H. Refusal to accept group intervention (help)
   a. Not responding positively to group intervention

I. Group support of negative behavior
   a. Refusal by group to correct behavior that is harmful to peers or the group process

J. Assault upon staff or peers

Any physical act that could be harmful to a staff person or peer

K. Weapons

Possession of any item that could be used in a harmful manner

L. Sexual misconduct

Any unlawful sex act

M. Non-Participation in program

Failing to participate in program without s

N. Inciting group misconduct

Any overt (or convert) act intended to disrupt the order and safety of program

H. AWOL

Leaving the building without permission, demonstrating a clear intent to truant by plotting or preparing material to truant

References

References;

Vorath, H. H., & Brentro, L. K. (1985). *Positive Peer Culture.* (2nd ed.). Hanthorne, NY: Aldine pg 46-50

"Mireillo Guiliano." BrainyQute.com Xplore INC, 2016, 26 December 2016. http://www.brainqute.com/quotes/m/Mireillegu530753.html

"Harry S Truman." BrainyQute.com Xplore INC, 2016, 26 December 2016. http://www.brainqute.com/quotes/author/h/herry_truman.html

"Thomas Aquinas." BrainyQute.com Xplore INC, 2016, 26 December 2016. http://www.brainqute.com/quotes/author/t/Thomas_Aquinas.html

"Mahatma Gandhi." BrainyQute.com Xplore INC, 2016, 26 December 2016. http://www.brainqute.com/quotes/authors/m/mahatma_gandi.html

"George Bernard Shaw." BrainyQute.com Xplore INC, 2016, 26 December 2016. http://www.brainqute.com/quotes/authors/b/benard_shaw.html

"Winston Churchill." BrainyQute.com Xplore INC, 2016, 26 December 2016.

http://www.brainqute.com/quotes/auther/w/winston_churchill.html

"Henry Ford." BrainyQute.com Xplore INC, 2016, 26 December 2016. http://www.brainqute.com/quotes/author/h/henryford.html

"Dr. Seuss." BrainyQute.com Xplore INC, 2016, 26 December 2016. http://www.brainqute.com/quotes/dr. seuss.html

"Albert Einstein." BrainyQute.com Xplore INC, 2016, 26 December 2016. http://www.brainqute.com/quotes/author/a/albert_einstein.html

"Bruce Lee." BrainyQute.com Xplore INC, 2016, 26 December 2016. http://www.brainqute.com/quotes/author/b/bruce_lee.html

"e. e. cummings." BrainyQute.com Xplore INC, 2016, 26 December 2016. http://www.brainqute.com/quotes/author/e/cummings.html

Other Sources:

Programing Handout; *Ideas to improve Group Functioning*; Generated at Group Work Training on December 9, 1998

Programing Handout; *Starting Group Meeting in a New Program; How will group meeting operate*; December 9, 1998

Programing Handout; *Twelve Strategy Development Questions*; Generated at Group Work Training on December 9, 1998

Programing Handout; *What to Look For in Groups*; from 1972 Annual Handout for Group Facilitators, University Associates, 1972, pp. 21-24.

Programing Handout; *G.V.R.C. New Youth Orientation Pamphlet;* revised on March 2004

NOTES:

www.ingramcontent.com/pod-product-compliance
Ingram Content Group UK Ltd.
Pitfield, Milton Keynes, MK11 3LW, UK
UKHW040600210726
13854UKWH00008B/1658